How Can I Deal With...

When People Die

Sally Hewitt

A⁺

Smart Apple Media

Smart Apple Media is published by
Black Rabbit Books
P.O. Box 3263, Mankato, Minnesota 56002

U.S. publication copyright © 2009 Black
Rabbit Books. International copyright
reserved in all countries. No part of this
book may be reproduced in any form
without written permission from the
publisher.

Printed in the United States

Published by arrangement with the Watts
Publishing Group Ltd, London.

Library of Congress Cataloging-in-
Publication Data

Hewitt, Sally, 1949-
    When people die / Sally Hewitt.
    p. cm.—(Smart Apple Media. How can
I deal with—)
    Summary: "Case studies and helpful
advice for kids who have experienced
death of a close loved one"—Provided by
publisher.
    Includes bibliographical references and
index.
    ISBN 978-1-59920-231-0
    1. Children and death—Juvenile
literature. 2. Grief in children—Juvenile
literature. 3. Bereavement in children—
Juvenile literature. I. Title. II. Series.
BF723.D3H49 2008
155.9'37—dc22
                            2007035714

Picture credits:
Andy Crawford: front cover inset, title
page, 9, 10
Caro/Topfoto: 19, 20.
Bob Daemmrich/Image Work/Topfoto: 28.
©Esbin-Anderson/Image Works/Topfoto: 6.
Willie Hill, Jr./Image Works/Topfoto: 11.
James Marshall/Image Works/Topfoto: 22.
Brian Mitchell/Photofusion: front cover
main.
Network Productions/Image
Works/Topfoto: 7.
John Powelll/Topfoto: 5.
Nancy Richmond/Image Works/Topfoto: 4.
Ray Roberts/Topfoto: 27.
Ellen Senisi/Image Works/Topfoto: 8, 12, 13,
15, 21, 23, 24, 25, 26.
Skjold Photographs/Image Works/
Topfoto: 18.
Jim West/Image Works/Topfoto: 16, 17.

Series editor: Sarah Peutrill
Art director: Jonathan Hair
Design: Susi Martin
Picture research: Diana Morris
Series advisor: Sharon Lunney

9 8 7 6 5 4 3 2 1

Contents

I Don't Know What's Happening!

Lola's grandma has died, but her family hasn't told her yet. They stop talking when she comes in the room. Lola feels worried and afraid.

Ewan's Story

Lola is my little sister. She keeps asking me, "Where's Grandma? What's happened?"

I want to tell her, but Mom and Dad say

Lola's too young to understand about Grandma dying.

But not knowing is making Lola feel unhappy.

Lola's Story

Grandma was staying with us because she was ill. Mom was taking care of her. One evening, there was lots of running about, whispering, and phone calls. No one would tell me what was happening. Mom asked me to stay in my bedroom.

I saw an ambulance from my bedroom window. They took Grandma away. Mom says Grandma isn't coming back, but she won't tell me why. What's happened to Grandma? Are they whispering because they don't want me to know that Grandma doesn't love us anymore?

5

What Can Lola Do?

Lola is worrying because she doesn't know what's happened to her grandma.
She can:

✔ tell her mom she is worried,

✔ ask why Grandma has gone away, and

✔ say not knowing is making her think frightening things.

What Lola Did

I told Mom I thought Grandma wasn't coming back because she didn't love us. So Mom gave me a hug and told me Grandma had died. I burst into tears because I'll never see Grandma again. Mom said Grandma loved us and her love will never leave us.

I feel a bit better, but I wish Grandma was still here.

Grandma's 70th Birthday

What Is Death?

Death is when someone's body stops working and can't be made better.

Death is a natural part of life. All living things—plants, animals, and people—grow older and die eventually. Living things don't live forever.

People die because their bodies get old and worn out. They die because they are too ill to get better. Sometimes people die because they have a very bad accident.

A dead body can't feel pain or know what's going on.

I Don't Want to Say Good-bye!

Tim finds it hard to believe his dad has died. He won't go to the funeral to say good-bye because he wants to think he will see his dad again.

George's Story

My friend Tim's dad died. Tim keeps talking about him as if he is still alive.

He got really angry with me when I said I was sorry about his dad.

Tim's Story

Dad hasn't been well for ages. He's had medicine and operations, and they've always made him feel better! But Mom says that Dad got too ill for the medicine to work anymore. She says Dad died.

I can't believe Dad died. I think, if I don't say good-bye to Dad and if I don't go to the funeral, he'll walk in the door again, smiling! I'm afraid if I say good-bye I really will never see him again.

What Can Tim Do?

It would help Tim to know that he won't see his dad again. He can:

✔ talk to his mom about it and listen to what she says,

✔ go to his dad's funeral and say good-bye, and

✔ write a good-bye letter to his dad.

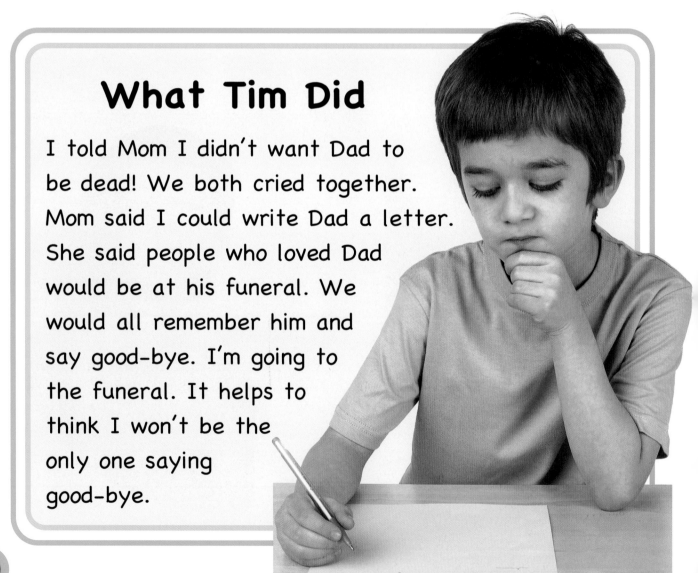

What Tim Did

I told Mom I didn't want Dad to be dead! We both cried together. Mom said I could write Dad a letter. She said people who loved Dad would be at his funeral. We would all remember him and say good-bye. I'm going to the funeral. It helps to think I won't be the only one saying good-bye.

What Happens at a Funeral?

Before the funeral, the body of the dead person is put in a box called a coffin. People can see the body at the funeral. Family and friends get together and remember the person and say good-bye. Many funerals are religious ceremonies.

After the funeral, the body is either buried in the ground or cremated, which means burned. The person's name is written on a gravestone, a plaque, or in a special book of remembrance.

I'm Angry with My Brother for Leaving Me

Wes's older brother Denny died in an accident. Wes feels angry with his brother for leaving him on his own and making his mom and dad unhappy.

Ricky's Story

Since Denny died, Wes is angry all the time—with Denny for dying and with his mom and dad about everything! He gets really angry if I talk about my big brother. I can't say anything right!

Wes's Story

A car knocked my big brother Denny off his bike and hurt him so badly he died.

I'm angry with Denny. I keep thinking he should have been more careful!

Now Mom and Dad are sad all the time. I can't talk about Denny because it makes them even sadder.

And they worry about me. They keep saying, "Be careful, Wes!" They won't let me ride my bike.

My friend Ricky's big brother is alive but mine is dead. It's not fair!

What Can Wes Do?

Wes's mom and dad feel sad and worried because of Denny's accident. Wes can talk to a grown-up he trusts. He can:

✔ say he feels angry with Denny,

✔ say he knows his parents worry about him, and

✔ say he doesn't like it when they think he is going to have an accident, too.

What Wes Did

I talked to Uncle Pete and he talked to Mom and Dad. Now they let me ride my bike in the park. I'm taking a cycling test so I can be safer when I ride on the road.

But I think Mom and Dad will always worry about me more because of what happened to Denny.

Will I Ever Stop Feeling Sad?

Vicki's mom died a year ago, but she often feels sad. She wonders if she will ever be happy again.

Joy's Story

Vicki is my friend. Sometimes when Vicki and I are having fun and she's laughing and happy, she suddenly gets sad and won't play anymore. I know she's thinking about her mom, but she won't talk about it.

Vicki's Story

On Wednesday it's the anniversary of Mom's death. It's a whole year since she died, but I still feel sad.

Every time I do something I used to do with Mom, I miss her and feel like crying because she isn't here anymore. I cried when Dad helped me make my birthday cake because Mom and I always did it together. Dad cried too.

Sometimes I forget that Mom died and I feel happy. Then I remember and I feel sad again.

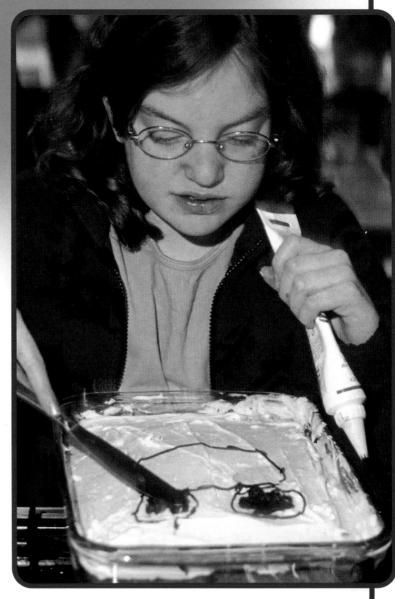

What Can Vicki Do?

Vicki will always miss her mom. It helps to have happy memories. She can:

✔ tell her friend Joy how she feels,

✔ talk to her dad, or

✔ plan something special on the anniversary of her mom's death.

What Vicki Did

I talked to Dad and he said he still feels sad too. We decided to make Wednesday a special day for Mom. We cooked her favorite meal, went on her favorite walk, and even told her favorite jokes! We'll always be sad that Mom died, but we don't always have to be sad when we remember her.

I'm Afraid I Will Die Too

Luke thought that only pets and very old people died. So when his friend Sid died, he was shocked. Now Luke is afraid of dying, too.

Amos's Story

Luke and Sid were my best friends. Sid died because he was very ill. Now Luke thinks he's going to die, too. But just because Sid died, it doesn't mean Luke or I am going to die.

Luke's Story

I was sad when my pet hamster died, and I cried when Grandma died. But I didn't worry because hamsters don't live for very long and Grandma was very old.

Then Sid died. He was only a kid like me! Now I think about dying all the time. I worry that Mom and Dad will die. I worry that I will die.

I can't get to sleep. When I do, I have nightmares. I go into Mom and Dad's room to make sure they are okay.

Amos keeps saying, "Of course you won't die!" He gets fed up with me. I don't want to tell Mom and Dad in case they get fed up with me, too. I wish I didn't feel so afraid.

What Can Luke Do?

Worrying about dying is making Luke unhappy.
He can:

✔ tell his mom and dad he is afraid of dying, and

✔ say he is afraid they will die.

What Luke Did

I told Mom and Dad. They said everyone has to die sometime, but there was no reason to think any of us would die soon. They said I must tell them when I feel afraid. But I don't feel so afraid now that I've talked to them. I do miss Sid though.

My Parents Don't Love Me Now

Nesta's mom and dad are sad that baby Sheri died. Nesta thinks they loved baby Sheri more than they love her.

Deena's Story

My friend Nesta told me her mom and dad talk about Sheri all the time. She thinks they wish she had died and not Sheri. She tries to be good so they will love her more. But I said, "Our moms and dads love us when we're good and when we're bad."

Nesta's Story

Sheri died when she was only a baby. Mom and Dad talk about how sweet and good she was. They say, "Sheri would have been a lovely girl."

I'm not sweet and good all the time. Sometimes I'm naughty. So I think Mom and Dad wish Sheri was alive instead of me.

I try to be good so they'll love me and be glad I didn't die. Sometimes I feel angry with Sheri. I feel bad about that.

What Can Nesta Do?

She can:

✔ remember that her mom and dad love her and they would be very sad if she died, and

✔ tell her mom and dad how she feels.

What Nesta Did

I told Mom and Dad I thought they wished it was me, not Sheri who died. I said I would try to be good. They gave me a big hug and said they loved me all the time—even when I was naughty.

Now that I know they love me, I'm not angry with Sheri any more.

I Miss Granddad Too

Brendan thinks no one knows how much he misses his granddad. Brendan's granddad was very popular with his family as well as his friends. They are all sad he died, but Brendan is very sad, too.

Ali's Story

I know my friend Brendan really misses his granddad. His mom, dad, aunts, and uncles all help each other when they feel sad. I try to help Brendan when he feels sad.

Brendan's Story

Granddad was my dad's father. Everyone loved him. He had lots of stories to tell, and he was kind and funny. He called me his "little pal" and we did things together.

When he died, everyone was sad—Dad, Mom, my uncles and aunts, and Granddad's friends. When they get together to remember Granddad, I feel left out.

I miss Granddad just as much as they do. I'm afraid if I talk to Dad or Mom about Granddad, it will make them sad all over again.

What Can Brendan Do?

He can:

✔ talk to his friend Ali,

✔ talk to his aunts or uncles, and

✔ tell them he misses his granddad and that he feels left out.

What Brendan Did

I talked to Ali. He said the grown-ups would understand that I missed Granddad too. So I talked to Granddad's sister. She is making a book with photographs and letters and stories about Granddad, and I'm helping her. We

put something new in the book when we feel sad about Granddad, and it helps us feel a bit better.

How Can I Remember Someone Special?

Someone who has died can always be part of you. Remember:

✔ special things they did and said,

✔ happy times together,

✔ games and jokes you shared, and

✔ books and television shows you both enjoyed.

You could also:

✔ make a photo album,

✔ make a box of memories to hold things such as a card they sent to you, a scarf they wore, or their favorite poem,

✔ help raise money for charity in their memory, or

✔ plant a tree for them and watch it grow.

When Our Friend Died

When Caitlin and Scott's friend Ruby died, they were shocked and very sad.

Caitlin and Scott's Story

Caitlin: When our dog Sandy died, I was really sad that I wouldn't see him again. I never thought the same could happen to one of my friends.

Scott: When Ruby died, I was really shocked. I thought only old people died.

Caitlin: Scott and I were Ruby's best friends. Ruby's mom and dad asked if we wanted to go to Ruby's funeral. I wasn't sure. I'd never been to a funeral.

Scott: Ruby asked me if I wanted to go. I wasn't sure either, but I'm really glad we went.

Caitlin: At Ruby's funeral, her mom and dad, her big brother, and our teacher all talked about Ruby and how special she was.

Scott: All the children in our class wrote something for Ruby. There were letters, poems, stories, and even jokes.

Caitlin: Her mom and dad read some of them aloud at the funeral. Then they put them with the flowers and cards people had sent.

Scott: Ruby's mom and dad said they were very pleased we had come to the funeral.

Caitlin: I felt really sad when I got home, and I cried. Mom gave me a hug and said I would begin to feel better, but it might take a long time.

Scott: At school, we planted a tree for Ruby. I think about her every time I see it.

Caitlin: Now we don't feel sad about Ruby all the time. We are often happy and have fun, but it doesn't mean that we have forgotten Ruby.

Glossary

Accident
Something that happens suddenly and unexpectedly. Some very bad accidents can hurt or even kill people.

Afraid
You are afraid when you feel worried about something bad happening.

Alive
People, plants and animals are all alive. When you are alive you move, eat, sleep, learn, and grow.

Ambulance
A van with special equipment that carries people to and from the hospital.

Anniversary
An anniversary is a date that is remembered every year because something important happened on that date.

Die
When someone dies, they are not alive any more.

Funeral
A service or ceremony held after somebody dies to honor and remember that person.

Miss
You miss someone when you feel sad that you don't see them anymore.

Sad
You are sad when you feel unhappy. When you feel sad, you sometimes want to cry.

Worry
You worry when you don't know what is going to happen and you think something bad might happen.

Further Information

For Kids:

http://www.kidshealth.org/kid/feeling/emotion/somedie.html
Learn about what happens when someone you know dies and how to understand what you're feeling.

http://kidsaid.com/
This site by kids, for kids, offers a safe place for kids to help each other deal with grief and loss. Experts will answer your questions, and kids can submit stories and artwork.

http://pbskids.org/itsmylife/emotions/death/
Lots of information about dealing with death, including stories from kids who have lost someone and how they dealt with it.

For Parents:

http://www.connectforkids.org/node/392
This Web site has many articles on helping kids cope with grief.

http://www.griefnet.org/
Griefnet is a community of people dealing with grief, death, or major loss. Support groups and resources for adults.

http://www.nmha.org/go/information/get-info/grief-and-ereavement
Mental Health America offers articles on dealing with grief and loss, and how to help children cope with grief.

For Teachers:

http://www.teachablemoment.org/toolbox/toughtimestoolbox.html
This site offers tips for addressing tough issues in your classroom and for helping kids express their feelings.

Index

Notes for Parents, Caregivers, and Teachers

Children can feel sad and confused when someone they love dies. They often don't really understand what has happened. There are many ways that adults can help children deal with their grief.

- Children need to know what has happened and that the person who has died will not come back.
- Being able to express thoughts and feelings is an important part of dealing with grief.
- Questions, doubts, and fears should always be taken seriously.
- It helps children to share happy memories of the person who has died.

Page 4 Lola's Story
Lola's parents think she is too young to be told her grandma has died. She thinks Grandma has gone away because she doesn't love her any more.
- Children need to be told plainly what has happened—that Grandma has died—not that she is asleep or gone away.

Page 8 Tim's Story
Tim doesn't want to go to his dad's funeral. He won't face the fact he'll never see his dad again.
- A funeral gives children a chance to share grief and happy memories with other people. Saying good-bye can help them accept what has happened.

Page 12 Wes's Story
When Wes's big brother was killed in a road accident, Wes was angry with his parents for worrying about him.

- It helps parents to remember that their grief over the death of a child can affect how they act toward their other children.

Page 15 Vicki's Story
Vicki is worried she will never stop feeling sad about her mother's death.
- An anniversary of someone's death can be turned into an opportunity to share happy memories.

Page 18 Luke's Story
Ever since his friend died, Luke has been worried about dying.
- Children need to know that everyone dies eventually. Understanding that early death is unlikely can help them to overcome fears and get on with normal life.

Page 21 Nesta's Story
Nesta is unhappy because she thinks her parents wish she had died, not her baby sister.
- Children need to know that they are special and that their parents love them for who they are.

Page 24 Brendan's Story
Brendan doesn't want to upset his parents by telling them how much he misses his granddad.
- Another member of the family or a friend can sometimes help children with their grief if the parents are too sad themselves.

Page 28 Caitlin and Scott's Story
Children could role-play the parts in this simple script and then discuss what happened.